Families

Cousins

Rebecca Rissman

Heinemann Library
Chicago, Illinois

www.heinemannraintree.com
Visit our website to find out
more information about
Heinemann-Raintree books.

To order:
☎ Phone 888-454-2279
🖥 Visit www.heinemannraintree.com
to browse our catalog and order online.

© 2011 Heinemann Library
an imprint of Capstone Global Library, LLC
Chicago, Illinois

Edited by Rebecca Rissman and Catherine Veitch
Designed by Ryan Frieson
Picture research by Tracy Cummins
Originated by Capstone Global Library Ltd
Printed and bound in China by Leo Paper Products Ltd

14 13 12 11 10
10 9 8 7 6 5 4 3 2 1

Library of Congress Cataloging-in-Publication Data
Rissman, Rebecca.
  Cousins / Rebecca Rissman.
    p. cm.—(Families)
  Includes bibliographical references and index.
  ISBN 978-1-4329-4656-2 (hc)—ISBN 978-1-4329-4664-7 (pb)
1. Cousins—Juvenile literature. 2. Families—Juvenile literature. I.
Title.
  HQ759.97.R57 2011
  306.87—dc22   2010016991

Acknowledgments
We would like to thank the following for permission to reproduce
photographs: Corbis pp. 7 (©LWA-Sharie Kennedy), 14 (©Heide
Benser); Getty Images pp. 6 and 8 (both Jupiterimages), 9
(Andersen Ross), 10 (Jack Hollingsworth), 11 (Camille Tokerud),
13 (Antenna), 17 (RPM Pictures), 18 (Tony Metaxas), 23 b
(Camille Tokerud), 23 d (Jack Hollingsworth); istockphoto pp.
5 (©Duane Ellison), 15 (©kzenon), 19 (©Linda Kloosterhof),
20 (©Carmen Martínez Banús), 22 (©Diane Labombarbe), 23 a
(©Carmen Martínez Banús); Photolibrary pp. 12 and 23 c (both
Kevin Dodge); Shutterstock pp. 4 (©Michael Jung), 16 (©Morgan
Lane Photography), 21 (©Kim Ruoff).

Front cover photograph of three children embracing with
permission of Getty Images (Sami Sarkis). Back cover photograph
of children in a tent reproduced with permission of Shutterstock
(© Morgan Lane Photography).

We would like to thank Anne Pezalla and Nancy Harris for their
invaluable help in the preparation of this book.

Every effort has been made to contact copyright holders of
any material reproduced in this book. Any omissions will
be rectified in subsequent printings if notice is given to
the publisher.

Contents

What Is a Family?

A family is a group of people. People in families are called

family members.

Family members care for one another.

All families are different.

All families are special.

What Are Families Like?

Some families are very large.

Some families are very small.

Who Are Aunts and Uncles?

Some families have aunts
and uncles.

Aunts and uncles are the sisters and brothers of parents.

Who Are Cousins?

Cousins are the children of aunts and uncles.

Cousins can be boys or girls.

Different Cousins

Some families have many cousins.
Some families have no cousins.

Some cousins live near by.
Some cousins live far away.

Some cousins look alike.
Some cousins look different.

Some cousins like the same games.
Some cousins like different games.

Some cousins live with their parents.

Some cousins live with different family members.

Some cousins are adopted.

They have joined a new family.

Do you have cousins?

Family Tree

Grandmother — Grandfather

Uncle — Aunt · Mother — Father

Cousin · You

Picture Glossary

adopted invited to a join a new family. Many children are adopted by new families.

aunt a parent's sister

cousin child of an aunt or uncle

uncle a parent's brother

Index

Note to Parents and Teachers
Before Reading
Open the book to page 22 and show children the family tree graphic. Explain to children that the lines connecting the different boxes represent relationships. Then use this graphic to explain how they are related to their parents, their grandparents, their aunts and uncles, and their cousins.

After Reading
Ask children to raise their hands if they have aunts or uncles. Then ask children to raise their hands if they have any cousins. Engage the class in a contest to see who has the most cousins. Ask children to raise their hand if they have one cousin, two cousins, three cousins, etc, until only one child has his or her hand raised. Ask this child how many cousins he or she has!